ISBN: 978-1-7357577-9-7

First edition.

Pamphlet

of

Hope

Jay Snider

Table of Contents

<u>Introduction</u>

I started this journey writing poems for the members of our small family church to provide comfort to our friends during challenging times. I was pleasantly surprised with the feedback I received and thought others might find value in these pieces. On the chance these poems provide a small measure of hope, I thought to create this little book.

My lifelong belief has been that we are at our best when we are providing optimism and love to others. During times of strife, this belief has been challenged. I wrote these poems as much for myself as anybody. Writing them helped me cope with life's hard times and be open to its opportunities. As is the case with many writings, the words on each of the following pages come from personal experiences. My journey has been a fulfilling one involving many blessings and many trials. I am learning to embrace it all, even the times that seem bleak, as they bring a chance for reflection and redirection of purpose. I have discovered that it is through my challenging times I have truly found myself and—just as important—discovered who I want to be.

I have been fortunate enough to experience many cultures throughout the world. Although born in the United States, my life began in Germany as my father was a civilian in the Army based in Heidelberg. This experience taught me the value of cultural, religious, and physical diversity early in life. Diversity comes in many forms, including thought and culture. There is a richness in diversity which I try to embrace and support each day.

I left Germany at the age of eight and spent my remaining years of youth in Maryland. I went to college in Ohio and, post-graduation, I decided to stick around. This turned out to be a lucky decision since I met my current wife at that time. We've been married since 2004, each year more blessed than the last. Together with our two beautiful daughters we have lived in the South, New England, and Midwest sections of the country. Within each region we have experienced various traditions, cultures, and views of the world. And yet with these differences we have experienced harmony and care. This has empowered me to see that there is always hope, even in the darkest of times.

In the spirit of spreading harmony, I offer these poems to you. May you find a sliver of encouragement in the message they bring. Each person's life journey is their own. Should we choose to do so, we can all have a role to play in spreading love and peace.

Jay Snider

Duck and the Pond

A man happened by
a small tranquil pond.

Much on his mind
As he walked along.

The air was still
a slight breeze on the cheek

A small hint of chill
that both tickled and teased

With questions on his mind
much went unnoticed.

Confused and quite anxious
he was narrow in focus.

"What am I to do?"
he kept on repeating,

"I have the world's problems,
and the weight is amazing."

"What to do about this?
What about that?"

No answers come to mind
just more confusion.

"I need all these answers.
I need them now!

Nothing is working.
My mind keeps spinning."

As he pondered and thought
he happened to see

A little brown duck
that was going downstream.

The sight was perfect
simple and captive.

Elementary, yet majestic
Nature's true canvas.

Although quite a setting
the man paused to look.

Unsure of the reason
something took hold.

This astounded man thought,
"Why do I stop?

My problems are many.
This duck has naught."

The man lost in thought
the duck lost in drift.

One discontent
the other quite captive.

"This duck can't have reason,
no clear objective.

No purpose to mind,
no resemblance of worth.

I see no value
to this duck's simple life.

But I can't help but feel
their heart is alive."

Where the stream fed the pond,
it finally made sense.

This duck had much purpose,
great value and reason.

In the pond was a family,
becoming entwined in glee.

Jubilation now together,
they embraced love's wings.

Reflecting on this,
the man turned with intention.

Love and family await me,
one focused direction.

No more time pondering worries,
off I go heading home.

Goodbye gentle duck,
time to spread wings of my own.

———

     I was inspired to write this poem by Henry Howard's "The Things That Cause a Quiet Mind." There is great truth in understanding and appreciating the simple things. As are knowing who you are and knowing where you are going, not concerning yourself with the many trials and doubts that can creep into your mind. Instead, try focusing on knowing what makes a life worth living for you and thus making life simple.

Clearing Away the Fog

We all have fears,
This I know,
Fear is a driver.
It likes to grow.

No listening occurs,
When fears run high.
Instead, we scream louder,
Though it makes others cry.

I know the tears well
I listen to the screams.
What happened to listening
To other's sweet dreams?

I think it is fear,
Causing this scene.
Fear lives inside,
Each of our beings.

But wait...
On further reflection.
Maybe there is more,
To this feeling of dread.

Yes, fear runs in circles,
We never get better.
Keep running, no path,
In panic, keep chasing.

But enough of this fear.
I am standing up to this now.
I am leaving this fog.
It is time to step out.

I have a new mantra,
A new voice that I follow.
"Love and hope" is for me,
So clear, so aspiring.

We all have our fears.
Of this I know.
No more fear, I choose love
And unceasing hope.

———

     Every journey in life has times of prosperity. There are also times of uncertainty when we feel dread and despair. We venture through a fog as we try to gain understanding and perspective on what is happening and what we can do to lift ourselves out of it. This poem came from a moment like that. There is no magic cure for feeling down, and I certainly do not have the right to say I understand anyone else's fog since it stems from their own experiences. But I have walked through my own fog before and will likely do so again.

A Walk in the Woods

I feel lost in the woods,
I am surrounded by doubt.
Each tree blocks the light.
I try to find my direction.

Should I give more to others?
Am I helping people at all?
I cannot tell what's enough.
I want to answer the call.

Am I being true to myself?
And what does "self" mean?
As I look in the mirror,
Do I like what I see?

What makes a good person?
What makes a good friend?
I have love in my heart.
Do I let it come out?

I continue to walk
As these thoughts keep going.
Challenging, poking,
They never stop slowing.

Still lost in the woods,
Raising my head, I see.
Many people in the world
Are tangled like me.

These people are not bad,

They have good in their hearts.
But just like me
They are lost in the dark.

Maybe while being lost,
I found greater than me.
Instead of the darkness
Provide others a gleam.

I am still lost in the woods.
But now that is fine.
A single light still has power
To make forests shine.

———

     I think there are moments in everyone's life where they stop and ask themselves if they are living as the person they want to be. A snapshot of themselves in the mirror asking if their beliefs, behaviors, and attitudes truly represent their ideal image. This is not asking about the meaning of life. Rather, this is asking if we're doing all we want in the life we've been given. If not, we can feel like we're mentally "lost in the woods." We struggle to find ourselves and who we want to be through the dense forest of our own wants and other people's unrealistic expectations. In those moments, we can sometimes find the greatest enlightenment and realization.

Living in a Pandemic

How do you wake, to face another day?
With feelings of isolation, unsecure, alone.
Shut in our homes and scared to leave.
A pandemic is here and broad is the reach.

Don't touch, don't hug, don't look around.
Don't look in someone's eyes.
Just look down.

Now our virus is political, as most things go.
Live your life, no stay in, who's to know?
How then to rise, awake and hope?
How to be happy and find strength to go on?

Maybe outside I will find the cure.
Inside myself, there is much to endure.
Peeking outdoors I see birds in flight,
Singing and soaring, their world hasn't stopped.

The sun still smiles as it starts to rise.
Colors paint the clouds
on my bright morning sky.

Flowers are still growing, I smell their perfume.
Life dances all around me, warm jubilation.

Peeking inside there is family and more.
Intimate smiles are with me, love endures.
Yes, we are trapped, but this is not strife.
Instead, there is much, I just had to look.
Now inspired by this, renewed hope is felt.

I turn now to those who also need help.
Supporting my neighbor,
supporting the stranger.
They are not all alone; I will help them believe.

The world needs love, for people to stand.
I will not let despair take over this land.
To all those in despair, remote isolation,
Look to me for a smile and warm salutation.

———

    The COVID-19 pandemic has hit everyone in the world and touched us all in unique ways. Isolation and loneliness have gripped many of us, even those who are surrounded by family. In the darkest of these moments, I looked for some ray of positivity, something to cling onto, to pull me out of the crisis. In doing so, I found not only hope, but also greater appreciation for life. And this appreciation has been a wonderful gift.

Through My Window

Sitting by my window I look to see
All of the wonders life can bring.

Trees grow tall, swinging with the wind
Buds burst open, it's springtime again.

Birds are in chorus and gaily fly by
Clouds in pastel colors dance in the sky.

Grass in our yard is starting to green
Hope and joy are alive, so simple a scene.

I look through my window and smile,
feeling alive
This world has much to admire.

———

I've found some of the most reflective and spiritually fulfilling times are when I sit back and look through a window. Not at anything in particular, simply sitting back and looking at all the natural world has to offer. Appreciating these little moments I wrote this simple poem. No real agenda or point other than to say "Thank you" for the world around us.

Time to Close My Window

Through my window I see pain,
There is much heartache out there.
I see people calling out,
It is time for change!

I see people justly angry,
They see what is wrong.
I see voices screaming loudly,
Trying hard to be heard.

I see peaceful protest,
They are linked in arms.
I see calls for justice,
And their beautiful song.

I see colors joining hands,
Spreading the message of love.
I see the songs for equality,
Raising to heavens above.

I start to see the inequity,
And the blatant mistreatment.
I see myself change,
It's time to speak against it!

Through my window I see hope,
But also a call,
Time to shut my window and demand
Justice, peace, and love for us all!

———

Taking time to enjoy all the beauty and wonder that exists in the world is a beautiful thing. But there are also times when we are called to action. Times when we need to close the window we look through and instead become a solution. We may not always know exactly what to do, but we know we need to answer the call.

My Daughter's Gift

I have a daughter,
Gifted from birth.
A talent that is hidden,
But can change you forever.

If you look at the surface.
Her mind is unique.
ADHD grabbed hold.
A special challenge unseen.

She can't catch your eye,
It appears lost in the distance.
Off in flight her stare goes.
But dancing eyes still listen.

Sometimes in speech,
Her message is wide.
A train of thought dissembles,
On the platform we wait.

Yes, when she speaks,
Thoughts go awry.
But try to pay attention,
Your heart just may fly.

For words are a power,
Both evil and good.
In her presence is felt,
Where angels once stood.

She speaks from the heart,
As her words quickly fly.
It is your choice to hear,
Or simply to pass by.

She is not alone,
And all are quite special.
They all have a voice,
Their own symphony of notes.

So please stop and listen,
To all the words she might say.
Not for her sake but yours,
You will be grateful one day.

I have a daughter,
Gifted from birth.
A talent that is hidden,
Found in her large heart.

———

One of my greatest gifts in life is being a father to not one, but two perfect girls. One of whom has ADHD. This condition has given her many talents, including a strong compassion for and love of the human condition. This poem focuses on one of the more obvious side effects of her ADHD, which is a struggle to form coherent speech. It can be hard to follow her conversation as her mind is going faster than her mouth can speak. In my view, it's also because her heart is trying to pour out so much love so quickly. A more caring person I've never found. I just wish others would take the time to listen to someone like her.

My Thanksgiving

What does it mean to be called a friend?
How does one show genuine affection?
How does one show they care?
What does it mean, to always be there?

Does it mean we give everything?
Expecting nothing in return.
Does it mean we truly listen?
Instead of our own troubles, focus on theirs?

Do we need similar tastes, likes, and interests?
Or do opposites attract,
And we benefit from difference?

Is it someone that ensures our back is covered?
Our best interests at heart; mutual respect.

For me a friend puts these questions to rest.
Outside of my family,
they are life's greatest gift.

They all have leading roles
in my personal play.

No part is too small; no line they say forgotten.

Thank you to all who have impacted my life.
Thank you to all who make things right.
You all are my friends making life worth living.
This poem is for you, my thanksgiving.

––––

On top of being a father, I've also been gifted with fantastic friendships. Friends are defined in many ways. Some friendships last a lifetime. Others seem to come about at just the right time in our lives, even though they're temporary. Regardless of the length of time we are given, the friendships we have are their own miracles. In my life, I have been blessed with many friends all over the world. In all its forms, friendship is a delight. This poem was meant for all those who have played a role in my life's journey.

www.ingramcontent.com/pod-product-compliance
Lightning Source LLC
Chambersburg PA
CBHW071808020426
42331CB00008B/2443